Solutions Series: Gross & Fine Motor Skills

ages 3–6

by

Marilee Whiting Woodfield

Published by Totline® Publications
an imprint of
Frank Schaffer Publications®

Author: Marilee Whiting Woodfield
Editor: Mary Rose Hassinger
Interior Designer: Robin Gale Wynsma

Frank Schaffer Publications®

Totline Publications is an imprint of Frank Schaffer Publications.

Send all inquiries to:
Frank Schaffer Publications
8720 Orion Place
Columbus, Ohio 43240

Solutions Series: Gross & Fine Motor Skills—ages 3–6

ISBN: 1-57029-529-8

3 4 5 6 7 8 9 10 QPD 12 11 10 09 08

Table of Contents

Introduction

After the toddler years of rapid growth and change, growth in preschoolers becomes more evenly paced. With this stability, and as their bodies become more proportionate, preschoolers begin to develop motor skills rapidly as they gain control of their bodies. Preschoolers like to test these new skills and stretch their abilities particularly when it comes to developing gross and fine motor skills.

What are gross motor skills?

Gross motor skills involve the large muscle groups, particularly in the arms, legs, back, and shoulders. These skills include activities such as running, throwing, kicking, and balancing on one foot. Coordination, strength, agility, and endurance are just a few of the gross motor skills developed through play centered around the large muscle groups. As preschoolers gain more control over these large muscle groups, their movements become smoother and more rhythmic.

A child's build affects his gross motor abilities. A child with long limbs will have better leverage for jumping and running. A child who is more muscular will have more power and endurance. A child with a stocky build will be less flexible and less agile. Recognizing these differences and planning activities that build on the strengths and challenge weaknesses will help you plan a varied movement curriculum that will benefit everyone.

What are fine motor skills?

Fine motor skills are movements or activities that are produced by smaller muscles or muscle groups. While there are many small muscle groups, typically preschoolers focus on fine motor skills in the hands and fingers. Activities such as building with blocks, drawing, and molding dough are activities that build fine motor skills. Dexterity, strength, eye-hand coordination, and visual discrimination are other skills that are enhanced through play experiences that address fine motor skills.

The importance of movement in your curriculum

Studies have shown that all experience in early childhood is critical to maximum brain development. Developing gross and fine motor skills is a part of this important development. Movement helps the organization of the brain. It reinforces growth and builds connections between different parts of the brain. More connections mean more brain power and more problem-solving power.

As children grow, they develop skills from the inside out and from the top down. This means, for instance, that a baby will be able to control his head before he can control his hands and his feet. A child will also develop skills with his arms before

Introduction (continued)

he masters those using his hands and fingers. This sequential growth means that new abilities are added as skills are mastered.

Children need opportunities to move and burn energy. They need opportunities to explore, stretch, and grow. Children need opportunities to exercise to keep their bodies healthy. As children engage in large motor activities, endorphins—a chemical released in vigorous exercise and relaxation—is released into the brain. Endorphins help you feel good, so planning curriculum where children have opportunities to run and move not only increases their muscle and motor abilities and gives physical release, but it makes them feel good.

Fine motor skills are essential to developing the coordination and hand strength needed for success in writing, cutting, other self-help skills such as buttoning and zipping, and eventually reading. The key is planning and organizing all this "learning." The easy part is that it's all just fun and games to the children. After all, learning through play is what they do best.

How to use this book

The fine and gross motor skills included in this book are organized by individual skill activities. For example all the activities for "block building" will be found together. Each individual activity is broken down into the various age levels so the fun progresses from simple to more complex skills. The number by each activity will let you know which skills are best for the children in your class or age group. Start with simple skills and work your way up to more challenging tasks as the children master new abilities.

Use the "Look What I Can Do!" skills sheets (pp. 8–11) to keep parents abreast of what their children are learning, and to help you assess where the children are developmentally.

The general skills and equipment lists (p. 7) and the fine motor activities (pp. 12–14) and gross motor activities (pp. 43–45) pages will give you ideas for activities when you aren't looking for a specific skill to master.

Each activity is designed to be non-competitive—everyone works at her own pace. You will also find hidden dimensions of learning in each activity so instead of just performing a gross or fine motor skill, you'll be learning letters, numbers, thinking and reasoning, as well as many other skills at the same time. The children won't care why you've planned as you have, they'll just be happy to be "doing," and you can be happy in knowing that you're maximizing their learning opportunities.

Guidelines for Play

As you direct the children in the gross and fine motor activities, here are some guidelines to consider:

Safety. Particularly when engaging in gross motor skills where a lot of movement is involved, it is important to keep safety a priority. Make sure that all equipment is maintained. Look for splinters, sharp edges, loose bolts, nails, or other areas where a child might get pinched or caught. Make sure the landing area is soft and won't cause injuries, and that the area is large enough or appropriate for the activity you have planned. When using small manipulative objects, be sure to observe the children closely so they don't end up putting things in their mouths.

Variety. Children learn best when there are multiple and varied avenues for learning. Plan activities that exercise a variety of skills and extend simple activities to include learning in additional areas such as adding a counting game to bouncing balls, or patterning skills to fine motor activities.

Pacing. Take it at the children's pace. If you can see that they've grown bored with an activity, move on. Or, if they're fatigued, change the activity or take some time to rest and regroup.

Development. Children develop at different rates. While one child may have mastered a skill, others may be just beginning. Challenge the children with new skills, but don't push beyond what is developmentally appropriate.

Persistence. Since children grow and develop so rapidly, don't give up if they can't do something on the first try. Without doing more than is developmentally appropriate, continue to work on and try new skills.

Organize. Make sure there are containers for small things, and space to store large toys safely. This way you can control what gets used for which activities, and you won't have to sort through a ton of stuff to get what you need. Staying organized will also help the children be able to clean up after themselves when an activity is completed.

Attention span. Limit lengthy fine motor activities. It is hard for most preschool-aged children to sit for long periods of time. Plan activities that don't require a lot of time sitting at a table doing one thing.

Define limits. Make sure you define the appropriate use and space limits for each activity. This way you'll be able to keep the beads on the table and the trikes where they belong without an argument.

nOoPpQqRrSsTtUuVvWwXxYyZz

General Skills: Activities and Equipment Lists

Fine Motor Activities

- Painting
- Pasting
- Writing
- Putting in/taking out
- Dressing up
- Manipulatives
- Playing musical instruments
- Cutting
- Stringing beads
- Creating collages
- Molding clay or play dough
- Pushing buttons
- Sorting
- Coloring
- Manipulating puzzles
- Woodworking

Fine Motor Equipment List

- Beads
- Blocks
- Buttons
- Construction toys
- Containers for filling
- Glue sticks
- Magnets
- Measuring cups
- Musical instruments
- Pencils, crayons, markers
- Play dough
- Puzzles
- Ring stackers
- Scissors
- Shape sorters
- Small tables and chairs

Gross Motor Activities

- Tumbling
- Sliding
- Crawling
- Throwing
- Walking
- Pedaling
- Running
- Dancing
- Climbing
- Catching
- Balancing
- Jumping
- Kicking
- Carrying
- Tiptoeing
- Swinging

Gross Motor Equipment List

- Balance beam
- Balls
- Boxes
- Cones
- Gardening equipment
- Hoops
- Jump ropes
- Jungle gym
- Large pillows
- Music
- Ride-on toys
- Slides
- Stairs
- Swings
- Trampoline
- Trikes

school is

Look What I Can Do! 25–36 Months

Child's Name ______________________ Age in Months __________ Date ____________

A fine and gross motor skills checklist.

Fine Motor Skills	Yes	No	Almost
Removes the wrapper from a piece of candy			
Turns pages in a book one at a time	✓		
Picks up tiny objects with thumb and forefinger	✓		
Puts tiny objects into a container	✓		
Makes a simple bridge of 3 block	✓		
Builds a tower of at least 6 blocks	✓		
Imitates a simple train made of blocks			
Folds a piece of paper in half			
Paints with some wrist action (dots, lines, circular strokes)			
Snips with scissors			
Holds crayon with thumb and forefinger			
Draws and recognizes circles			
Scribbling becomes more deliberate			
Strings 3 one-inch beads			
Holds a small cup in one hand			
Pours from a small cup			
Brings spoon or fork to mouth, palm facing up			
Unbuttons large buttons			
Undresses and dresses with assistance			
Rolls, pounds, squeezes, and pulls clay			
Assembles a three-piece puzzle			
Gross Motor Skills			
Moves ride-on toys without pedals			
Throws a small ball underhand			
Catches a ball with straight arms in front of body			
Kicks a ball forward	✓		
Walks 2–3 steps on a balance beam			
Balances on one foot for several seconds			
Bends over without falling			
Walks backward 10 or more feet			
Runs forward well			
Walks on tiptoes a few seconds			
Pulls wheeled toys by a string			
Climbs stairs (two feet to each step)			
Jumps in place two or more times			
Jumps backward			
Jumps forward on both feet 8–14 inches			

Comments on back.

Look What I Can Do! 37–48 Months

Child's Name ______________________ Age in Months __________ Date ____________

A fine and gross motor skills checklist.

Fine Motor Skills	**Yes**	**No**	**Almost**
Screws and unscrews jar lids, nuts, and bolts			
Builds a tower of 6 or more blocks			
Copies a circle, vertical, and horizontal lines			
Smears or daubs paint			
Uses scissors			
Makes a continuous cut across a page			
Holds a pencil or crayon with fingers			
Colors with control			
Imitates a vertical line with a crayon on paper			
Strings beads on a shoelace			
Holds spoon in fingers with palm up			
Stabs food with a fork			
Serves self at table with little spilling			
Brushes teeth			
Zips and unzips jacket			
Puts shoes on			
Manipulates clay (rolls balls, snakes, etc.)			
Completes a 5–6 piece puzzle			
Gross Motor Skills			
Climbs on a jungle gym			
Uses slide independently			
Kicks a ball forward			
Kicks a rolling ball			
Throws a ball underhand 9'			
Catches a bounced ball			
Walks downstairs one foot on each step			
Stands on one foot for two or more seconds			
Bends over without falling			
Runs around obstacles			
Runs easily			
Walks smoothly forward, backward or sideways			
Stands on tiptoes a few seconds, can walk			
Pushes and pulls wheeled toys			
Jumps over a 6" barrier with both feet			
Jumps off a 2' object with both feet and lands with both feet			
Jump ropes 2 cycles			
Hops in place on one foot			

Comments on back.

Look What I Can Do! 49–60 Months

Child's Name ______________________ Age in Months __________ Date _____________

A fine and gross motor skills checklist.

Fine Motor Skills	Yes	No	Almost
Pours liquid into a glass			
Builds a tower of 10 or more blocks			
Creates a bridge of blocks from a model			
Draws a person with four or more body parts			
Draws a house			
Draws circles and squares			
Colors within lines			
Completes a simple maze			
Tries to write name			
Begins to copy some capital letters			
Cuts on a straight line			
Strings beads on a shoelace			
Butters bread with a knife			
Uses spoon and fork skillfully			
Puts on socks with proper heel placement			
Puts shoes on			
Manipulates clay to create animal and human forms			
Completes a 7–10 piece puzzle			
Gross Motor Skills			
Somersaults			
Gallops			
Throws overhand			
Kicks a ball forward			
Catches a bounced ball			
Catches a large thrown ball			
Stands on one foot 8 seconds			
Touches toes without bending knees			
Rides a trike skillfully			
Walks backward toe-heel			
Moves forward and backward with agility			
Walks a short distance on tiptoes			
Balances on tiptoes for 10 or more seconds			
Moves large objects by pushing and pulling			
Walks upstairs and downstairs without support			
Hops forward on one foot 3 or more times			
Hops on one foot up to five seconds			

Comments on back.

Look What I Can Do! 60+ Months

Child's Name ______________________ Age in Months __________ Date _____________

A fine and gross motor skills checklist.

Fine Motor Skills	**Yes**	**No**	**Almost**
Copies simple block patterns containing 10 blocks or more			
Draws pictures that represent things			
Cuts out a circle following a line			
Writes own name			
Draws a person with head, arms, legs, and trunk			
Copies circle, square, cross, and capital letters VTHOXLYUCA			
Stays within the lines when coloring			
Strings beads on a shoelace			
Uses a fork and spoon			
Unties an apron (behind self)			
Dresses and undresses without assistance			
Ties shoelaces			
Manipulates clay to create animal and human forms			
Completes a 10–15 piece puzzle			
Gross Motor Skills			
Somersaults			
Skips			
Pumps self on swings			
Climbs			
Moves rhythmically to music			
Catches bounced or thrown balls			
Throws balls overhead			
Balances on either foot for 10 seconds			
Stands on one foot with eyes closed without loosing balance			
Bends and touches toes without bending knees			
Rides a trike skillfully			
Runs			
Gallops			
Walks backward, toe touching heel			
Balances on tiptoes for 10 or more seconds			
Moves large objects by pushing and pulling			
Walks down stairs, alternating feet			
Jumps rope			
Jumps over knee-high obstacles			
Hops forward on one foot 5 or more times			

Comments on back.

Fine Motor Activities

Any activity that encourages children to use their fingers and hands in manipulating objects is a fine motor activity. These build coordination, dexterity, and strength. Fingerplays, turning pages in books, screwing lids on and off jars, hammering nails, peg boards, geoboards, water and sand tables, sorting, pouring, and pinching are all examples of fine motor skills. The following are some sample fine motor skills to get you started in planning activities for fine motor growth in your every day curriculum. Each activity can easily be adapted to every level of preschool development.

Sugar Blossoms

Prepare your favorite sugar cookie recipe. Have the children help you measure and mix the batter. Separate the dough and have children roll each piece into a $1\frac{1}{2}$" ball. Place the balls on a greased cookie sheet. Next have children remove the wrappers from chocolate kiss candies. Press one chocolate kiss into the center of each ball of dough. Bake as directed on the package.

Story Time

Set several large pillows or beanbags in a corner with several dolls and stuffed animals so that there are enough to share among 3 or 4 children at a time. Have the children take turns reading picture books to their stuffed animal friends, or to one another. Encourage the children to hold the dolls on their laps and to make up stories that go along with the pictures as they turn the pages one at a time.

Bean Sort

Practice picking up small objects with the thumb and forefinger by sorting beans. Place a variety of dried beans into a large container. Have the children scoop out a cupful and place the beans on a table for sorting. Place all the beans of each kind into separate piles until all the beans have been sorted. Encourage the children to count each variety of bean and ask them to tell you how they sorted the beans.

Extend this activity by making a beanbag out of the sorted beans. Drop beans one or two at a time into a sock until the foot of the sock is full. (It may be helpful to turn down the top of the sock to make it easier to fill.) Tie a knot in the sock to keep the beans inside. Decorate the outside as desired and use your beanbag for tossing and catching practice.

Where's My Top?

Provide a large assortment of plastic bottles and their lids in a bin. Have the children sort through the lids and bottles to see if they can match the top to the bottom.

Oo Pp Qq Rr Ss Tt Uu Vv Ww Xx Yy Zz

Fine Motor Activities (continued)

On the Job

Having opportunities to use woodworking tools develops fine motor skills. Provide safety goggles and aprons for the children to wear. Encourage children to tap small brads into a soft piece of wood using a child-sized hammer. (Alternative: use foam bricks for wood and golf tees for nails.) Let the children use sandpaper to smooth down pieces of wood. Don't forget to paint your construction masterpieces. Many construction toys with screws, nuts, and bolts are available commercially and are a great addition to your manipulative collection.

Typing

While they may not be proficient enough to type 60 wpm, or even have hands big enough for proper placement on a keyboard, providing children with opportunities to type letters and numbers on a typewriter or computer keyboard enhances fine motor skills as well as number and letter recognition. Have the children see if they can type all the letters in their name, or pull lettered blocks out of a box and find and type the letters they draw. If using a computer, size the font so it is large enough that the child can print out his work and copy the letters in his own handwriting.

Musically Inclined

Triangles, drums, sticks, wood blocks, bells, and xylophones all provide lots of fine motor stimulation in addition to sensory and rhythm skills. Play some marching music. Let the children tap and toot along. Make maracas out of beans and empty yogurt containers, drums out of sticks and empty tin cans, or castanets out of bottle caps glued to small elastic bands.

Finger Dancing

Place small stickers on the fingernails of two fingers. Play some music and dance with your fingers on the tabletop. Move to the floor, on top of a box of toys, your knees, etc. What is the difference in sound or feel each time you dance on a different surface?

Puppets

Manipulating the mouths and arms of puppets is a great way to strengthen the hand muscles and express creativity. Provide a large assortment of puppets and a small puppet theater (throw a blanket over a table or clothespin a blanket between two chairs). Have the children take turns doing simple puppet shows for one another.

Fine Motor Activities (continued)

Sawdust Pennies

Fill the sand table or a large bin with sawdust. Add several pennies or other similar small objects. Invite the children to sort through the sawdust to find the pennies hidden inside. Have the children count the pennies and see how high they can stack the pennies.

Extend this activity by adding a specific number of pennies to find, or by placing several small objects that belong in a category into the sawdust. For example, several small farm animals could be added to the sawdust. Once the child finds all the animals, have them guess how all the objects are related (all farm animals, all kinds of blocks, all the same color).

Magnets

Children are fascinated by the seemingly magical power of magnets. Provide an assortment of magnets and items that can be attracted to magnets along with an assortment of items that cannot be attracted to magnets. Have the children sort all the objects in the collection into two piles.

Extend the magnet play by adding lettered magnets to your magnet assortment. Have the children spell their names or other words they know with the magnets on a magnet board. Have them choose a lettered magnet. Have them find an object in the room that begins with the same letter.

Fingerprint Detectives

Exercise small muscles and get the room cleaned all at once! Fill a spray bottle with water. Add a few drops of mild dish washing soap. Remind the child that the sprayer goes only on walls and tables, not on people, books, or carpet. Arm the child with the sprayer and a small sponge or paper towel and set him off on an adventure to find fingerprints. Once he finds a dirty spot, let him spray it with the cleaner, and wipe it clean with the sponge.

Hide and Seek Surprises

Place a small toy, sticker, or other reward in a small container with a lid. Place this container inside a larger container, and these containers in an even larger container. Be sure to use containers that have a variety of lift-off or screw-on lids. Hide the container inside a closet. Give the child clues where to find his prize then let him twist, pull, and pry his way into his treat.

Oo Pp Qq Rr Ss Tt Uu Vv Ww Xx Yy Zz

Block Activities

24-35 Months
- Builds a simple bridge of three blocks
- Builds a tower of at least six blocks
- Imitates a simple train made of blocks

36-47 Months
- Builds a tower of six or more blocks
- Builds a bridge of three or more blocks

48-59 Months
- Builds a tower of ten or more blocks
- Creates a bridge from a model

60+ Months
- Copies simple block patterns containing ten blocks or longer

Manipulates Construction Toys

Blocks are important for preschoolers because they are so versatile. You can stack and build in any way you please. They can become anything from a fence around a barnyard, to a car, or a telephone. Stacking blocks reinforces spatial relationships, fractions, and ratios. They also let a child experiment with balance, cause and effect, and gravity. Whether you are working with small cubes, large wooden blocks, or cardboard bricks, playing with blocks strengthens the hands and fingers as they manipulate each block into place. Build towers, bridges, and trains as basic block activities, then try the following activity suggestions.

[2] Over the Bridge

Create a simple bridge of three blocks. Have a few small plastic action figures "walk" over the bridge to the other side. Count each figure as it crosses over the bridge. Once everyone is on the other side, have the child build a similar bridge and have him help the figures back over as he counts each one.

[2] Hide and Seek Blocks

Find a special block, or wrap a block in patterned paper. Place a trail of blocks across the room to a secret hiding place on the other side of the room. Deposit the special block at the end of the trail in the hiding place (behind the book shelf, under a pillow, etc.). Have the child start at one end of the block trail and pick up the blocks, putting them in a bucket as she moves from one end to the other. When she reaches the final block, have her create a trail for you or another friend to follow.

Block Activities (continued)

[3] Block "Writing"

Write each child's name on a strip of card stock. Using blocks with alphabet letters stamped on the sides, have the child "write" his name with the blocks by matching the letters on the card to the letters on the blocks.

[3] Block Trails

Create Block Pattern Cards by copying pages 17-18. Color as desired, separate along the dotted lines, and laminate for durability. You may wish to make several sets of cards. Have the children set three to ten cards (depending on age) in a row on the floor. Now make a block trail that mirrors the cards that have been set out. For example if the square, rectangle, and circle block cards have been laid on the floor, then the child would place a square, then rectangle, and finally a circle block in the same order. Continue creating block trails and figures by adding and changing the cards.

[4–5] Towering Heights

Create towers of blocks by rolling a die to see how many blocks must be in each tower. If you roll a "5," then the tower should be five blocks high. Repeat several times as time and interest allows.

Extend the activity so that each time the die is rolled, that number of blocks is added on top of the first set. Continue rolling and stacking until the tower falls and play begins again. How many blocks tall is a book? How many blocks tall is a toy fire truck? Stack the blocks in a tower to measure a variety of objects in the room. Which object is the tallest, or has the highest tower? Which is the shortest, or has the smallest tower? Which objects are about the same size?

Extend the block measuring activity and create a graph of the number of blocks used for each object measured.

[4-5] Block Patterning

Create block patterns by placing the blocks in order by colors, sizes, or other categories. Start with simple ABAB patterns and continue to expand to more complex patterns such as AABB, or ABB, ABC, etc.

Use the Block Patterning Cards (pp. 17–18) and see if the children can create the geometric figures using blocks.

Block Pattern Cards

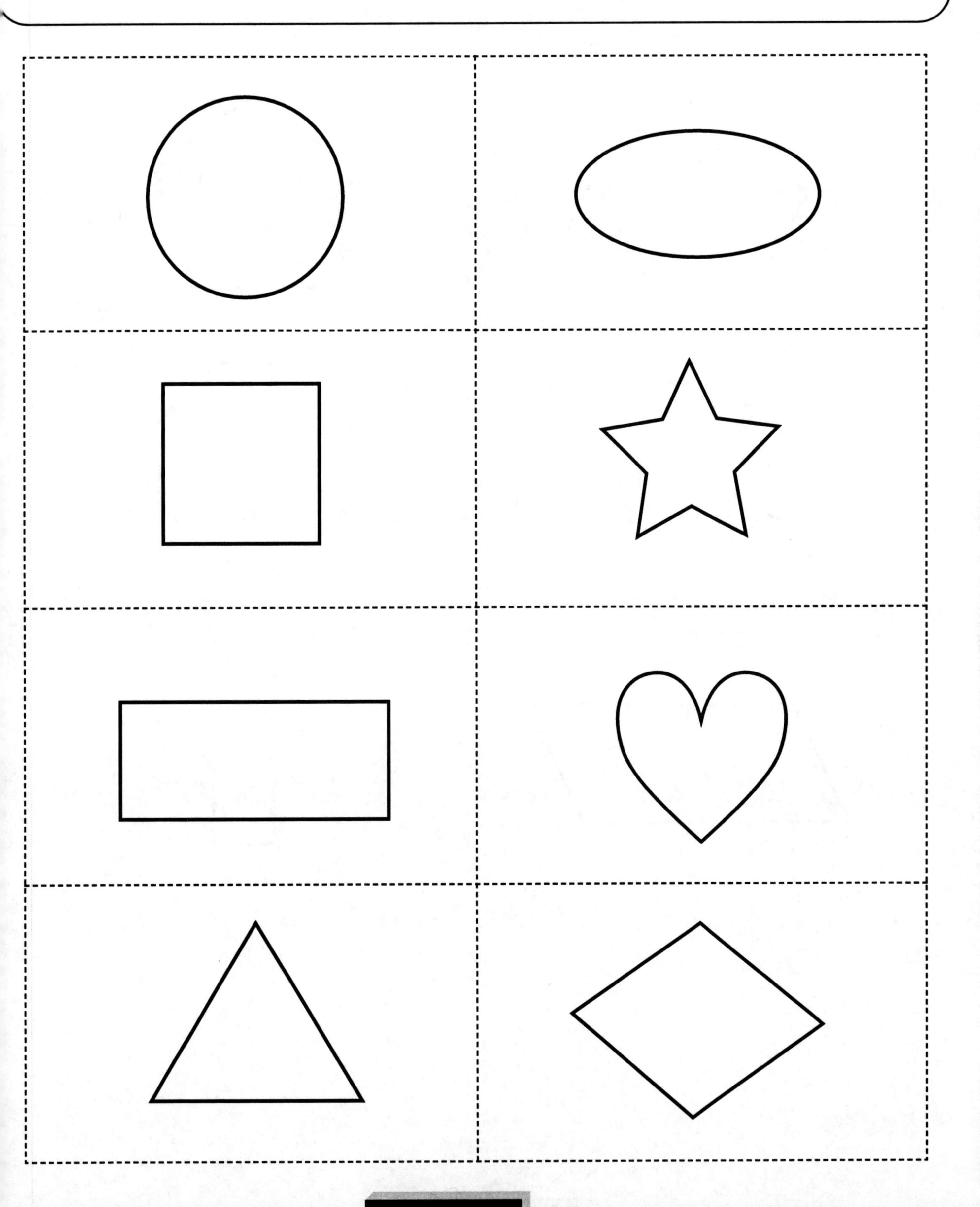

Block Pattern Cards

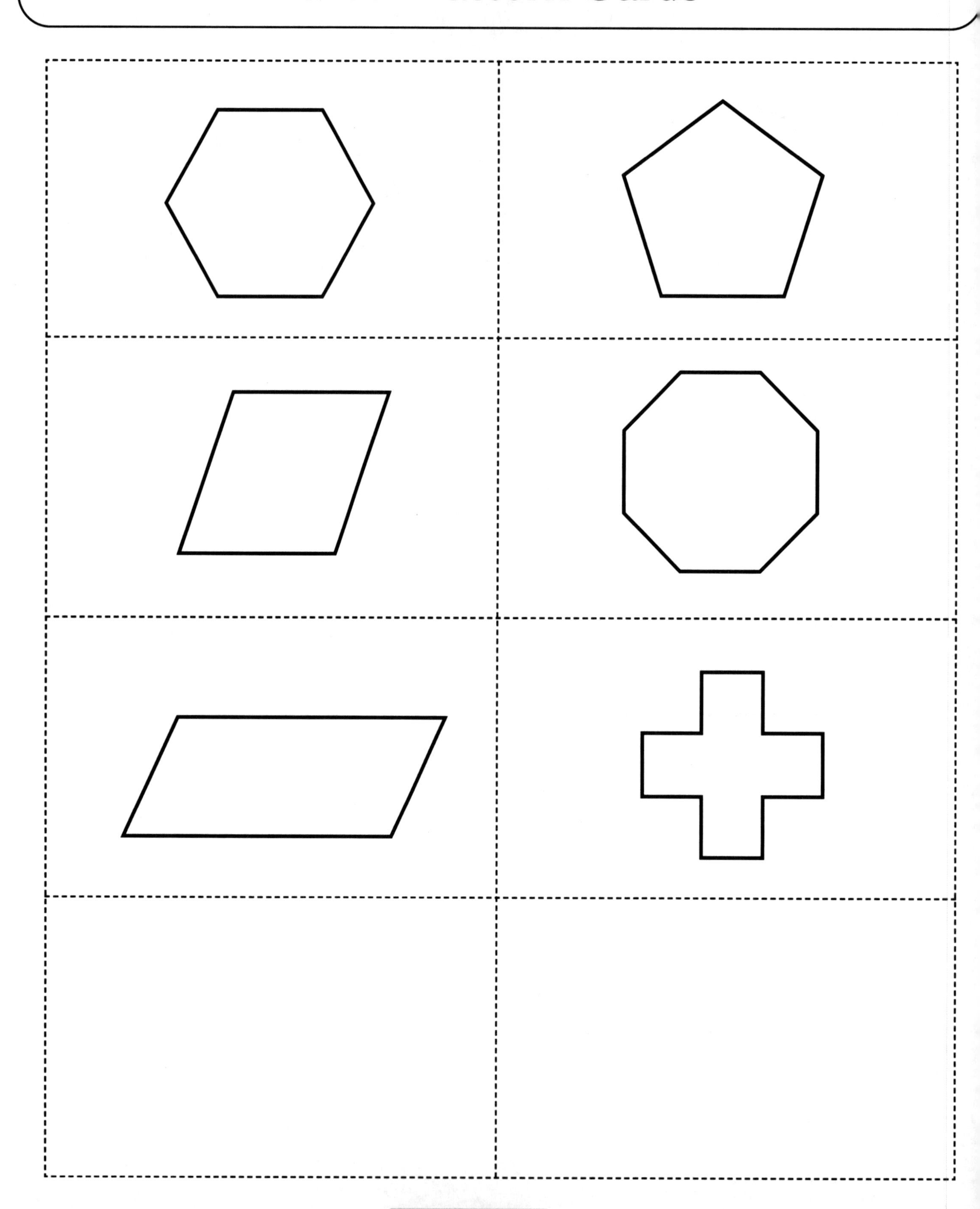

Arts & Crafts

24-35 Months

- Folds paper in half
- Paints with some wrist action (dots, lines, circular strokes)
- Snips with scissors

36-47 Months

- Smears or daubs paint (Draws or paints in vertical, horizontal, and circular motions)
- Draws a person with two to four body parts
- Uses scissors
- Makes a continuous cut across a page
- Cuts on a straight line

48-59 Months

- Draws a person with four or more body parts
- Draws a house (using geometric shapes)
- Cuts on a straight line

60+ Months

- Cuts out a circle following a line
- Draws a person with head, arms, legs, and trunk
- Draws pictures that represent things

Arts and crafts are a great way to enhance fine motor skills. Not only are little fingers bending, twisting, pinching, and pulling, they're also engaged in color, texture, and a variety of crafting mediums to create wonderful masterpieces.

As a child grows and becomes adept at many fine motor skills, you'll find that using scissors is a skill that runs the spectrum. Using scissors to cut on a line is one of those developmental skills that helps prepare children to read. You'll find the beginning efforts slow, awkward, and fairly unproductive. You will have to help a child learn not only how to hold a pair of scissors, but also how to pull them open and close them down on a piece of paper. It sounds easy enough, but can be a daunting and frustrating experience for little hands. Try sitting the child in your lap and holding paper for him while you remind him to pretend that the scissors are alligator jaws. Open wide, then "CHOMP" them closed. Let them practice on and shred scrap papers. Being able to cut freely will cut down on the frustrations of trying to follow a line in the first stages of cutting. As she gains control, remind her to turn the paper, not the scissors for an easier cutting job.

Creating collages is a great activity for all preschool ages because collage work adapts itself to each individual. Young preschoolers will need help with the glue, but let them tell you where they want it put. Provide lots of different materials including noodles, dried beans and lentils, cut straws and chenille stems, sequins, yarn, tissue paper, stickers, leaves, cotton balls, and any other assortment of small items.

Arts & Crafts (continued)

Allow opportunities for plenty of painting and drawing. You'll see paintings go from random strokes and garbled colors, to beautiful creations that are recognizable (even if the sky is orange and the trees are purple). Provide opportunities to paint on a grand scale as well as with smaller tools on smaller paper. You'll see self-portraits turn from a misshapen circle to creations with bodies, arms, legs, and even an occasional belly button. (Use the Self-Portrait Pattern (p. 24) for framing the children's self portrait creations.)

[2] Wee-Little Painting

Provide several small cups of paint (you can scent them by using liquid extracts if desired) and a handful of cotton swabs for each artist. Let them create masterpieces by using a wee-little cotton swab for a paintbrush.

[2] Stamping

Stamping is a fun activity for preschoolers. Provide lots of paper, a variety of stamps, markers, and washable ink. Have the children identify or tell a story about each stamped creation they create. Use cookie cutters, potato stamps, vegetables, and other unique surfaces for stamping and printing tools.

[2] Glue-Glop

Typically a bottle of glue in a young preschooler's hands is cause for concern. With this activity, however, little hands have the opportunity to squeeze and create. Not only is it tons of fun, it is also a very soothing activity to watch the glue drip and drizzle onto the paper.

Gather several small glue bottles. Add a teaspoon of tempera paint—a different color in each bottle. Stir with a craft stick. Open the tip of the bottle so that just a small stream can come out at once.

On a white piece of paper, let each child choose a colored glue bottle and watch it swirl onto the paper as they squeeze the bottle over the paper. Encourage them to move the bottle around and watch the patterns they are creating.

[3] Starch String Twists

Gather an assortment of different colors of yarn. Cut the strings into a variety of lengths 2-12" long. Have the children dip the yarn, one strand at a time into a bowl of liquid starch until the strand is completely saturated. Take the yarn and squeeze some of the starch out. Place the yarn on a piece of paper. Arrange the yarn as desired and repeat with a second string. As the starch dries, the yarn strands will harden in their twisted states.

Arts & Crafts (continued)

[4] Wiggly Squiggly Sculpture

Provide each child with a 4" foam ball that has been cut in half. Place the ball flat side down on the table. Cut several different colors and sizes of chenille stems. Allow the children to bend the chenille stems in any way they please. Have the children stick the twisted chenille stems into the foam ball to create a free-form wiggly, squiggly sculpture.

[4] Colored Rice Mosaic Creations

Place one cup of long grain rice (not instant) into a zippered plastic bag along with a few drops of food coloring and one Tbsp. of rubbing alcohol. Shake vigorously until the color is disbursed over the rice. Spread the rice on a sheet of waxed paper to dry. Repeat with other colors as desired.

Thin glue by pouring it into a small cup and adding just enough water so that the glue can be "painted" with ease. Have the children paint a patch of glue on their papers. Then pinch and sprinkle the desired color rice onto the glue. Continue gluing and pinching until the entire paper is covered.

[4] Rug Bugs

Use the Bugs in the Rug pattern page (p. 22) to practice cutting skills. Duplicate the bugs to fill a sheet of paper and make several copies. Cut out each bug around the dotted frame. Have the children decorate or color their rug as desired. Using scissors cut the rug out around the solid border. Attach the rug to a second sheet of paper by spreading glue along the top edge, making a sort of pocket. Have the children choose a handful of bugs. Color each one as desired. Lift the rug and paste the bugs under the rug. Write, "How many bugs under the rug?" on the paper. Have the child count the bugs he has hidden under the rug. Help him write the number of bugs he has hidden under his rug on his paper.

[5] Cut and Stack

Provide several sheets of paper with small, medium, and large circles, triangles, and squares printed or traced for each child. Have them cut out the shapes that are similar and paste them on top of one another in descending order (largest on the bottom). Encourage the children to fill a whole page of concentric circle stacks, or triangle stacks for a psychedelic page.

[5] Cut Me Home

Use the "Cut Me Home" pattern page (p. 23) to help practice cutting skills.

Bugs in the Rug

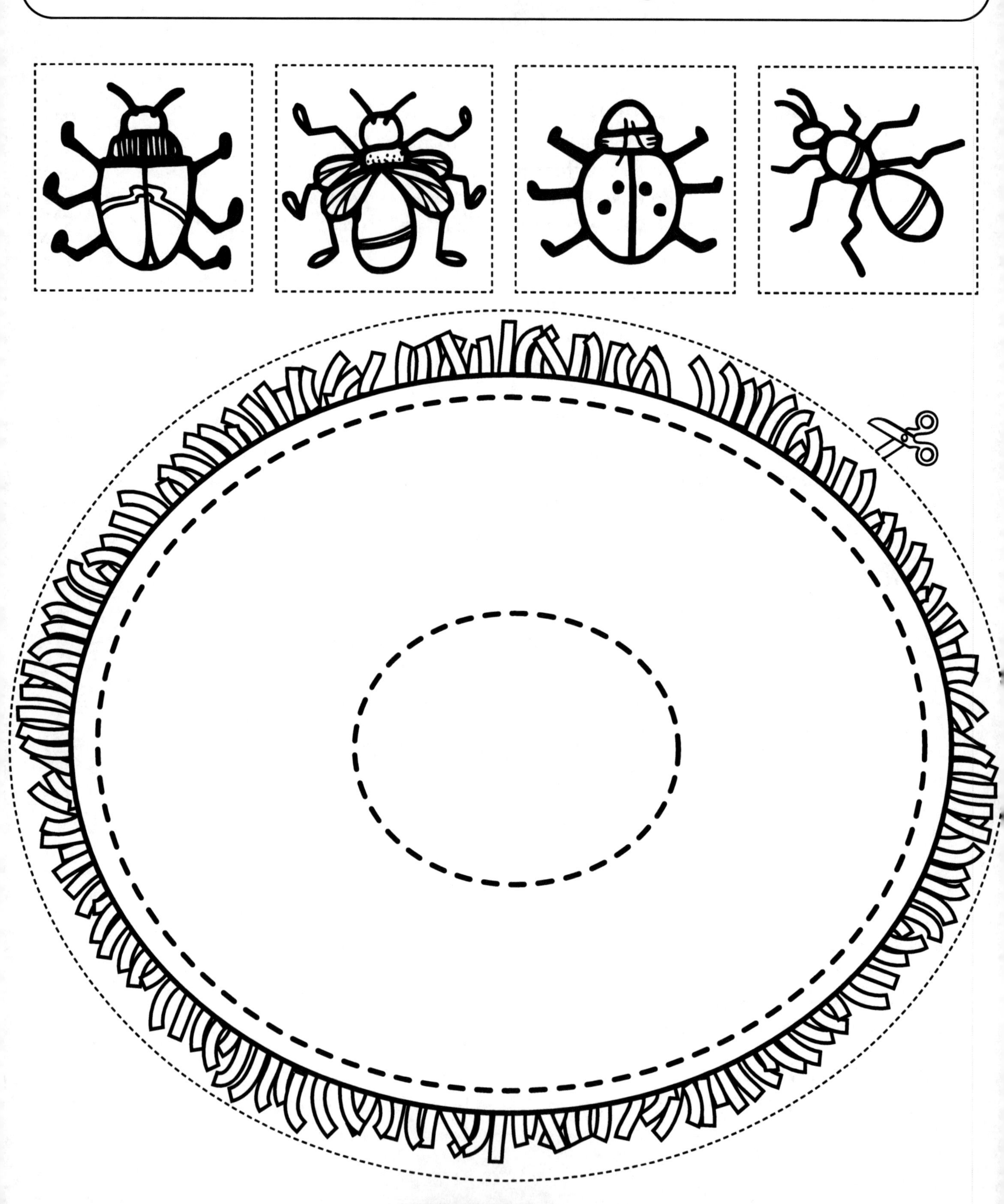

1-57029-529-8 *Solutions Series: Gross & Fine Motor Skills*

Cut Me Home

Self Portrait

Writing Skills

24-35 Months

- Holds a crayon with thumb and forefinger
- Draws and recognizes circles
- Scribbling becomes more deliberate

36-47 Months

- Holds pencil or crayon with fingers
- Colors with control
- Imitates a vertical line with a crayon on paper
- Copies a circle, vertical, and horizontal line

48-59 Months

- Draws circles and squares
- Colors within lines
- Completes a simple maze
- Tries to write name
- Begins to copy some capital letters

60+ Months

- Writes his own name
- Copies circle, square, cross, and capital letters: VTHOXLYUCA
- Stays within the lines when coloring

Learning to hold a pencil or crayon correctly and then using it skillfully is one of the major tasks of the preschool years. As fine motor skills develop, children will move from a tight-fisted grip on a crayon, to the more traditional hold between the thumb and fingers. To help young children maintain this proper hand position, it may be helpful to remind them to "pinch" the pencil and then let it rest on the third finger. It may also help to have the child cradle a cotton ball in their hand while holding the pencil properly to help maintain the grip.

Allowing for lots of opportunities to color, write, and draw will help children gain more confidence with writing. Let the children experiment with many different kinds of writing tools such as ball point pens, markers, crayons, pencils, colored pencils, and chalk. Always encourage each child to write their own name on their paper, even if all they know is their first initial. Utilize quiet times such as after naptime, to quietly color and draw. Have the children experiment with their coloring by using more than one color at once, using both hands at once, or by taping the paper to the underside of a table and coloring "upside-down" for variety.

Use the Copy Cat pattern (p. 27), "I Can Write My Name" (p. 28), and the Maze (p. 29) to help assess the skills listed above. Dot-to-dot pages, writing letters, and coloring are all activities that help children practice fine motor writing skills. In addition to the skills and activities listed above, here are some activities to enhance writing skills.

Writing Skills (continued)

[2] Do-It-Yourself Dot-to-Dots

Using washable ink and a pencil eraser, have the child create several dots on a piece of paper by dipping the pencil eraser in the ink and pressing it onto a paper. Once the child is satisfied with the number of dots he has created, turn the pencil over and draw lines between all the dots until they are all connected to one another. Have the child take a look at the criss-crossed creation to see if he sees an object in the outline. Have the child dictate what he sees in his dot-to-dot. Write his words on the bottom of the page.

[3] Scribble Chasing

This is a fun activity to do with a friend. Place a large sheet of craft or construction paper on the floor. Have each child choose a different color crayon for this activity. Select one child to be "it" and the other child to be the chaser. The first child draws a path on the paper with his crayon for the second child to follow with his crayon. Select two new crayon colors and go again. Continue creating paths and chasing until your page is completely covered with scribble chasing. Swap partners and play again.

[3] Doodle Music

Record a collection of three or four pieces of music. Make sure the pace or tone of each is distinct and unique. Some suggestions might be an up-beat children's song, a classical lullaby, marching music, and a dance tune. Give each child a handful of crayons and a large sheet of paper. Tell them you want them to doodle to the music. When the music tempo is fast, have them color quickly. When the tempo slows, have the children slow their coloring to match the new tempo.

[4] Texture Writing

Give each child a piece of paper and a crayon. Have them place their paper on a table to write their names. Next move to the carpet and have the children write their names again. Now move out to the playground and use the sidewalk, bricks, or siding for a third texture for writing. Continue seeking out different textures and writing names. When you are finished, compare each of the different textures. Invite the children to tell you which one they like best and why. Which one was easiest to write on? Which was the most difficult and why?

[5] Scribble Mural

Read *Harold and the Purple Crayon*, by Crockett Johnson, (Dark Horse Comics, 1981). Cover an entire wall with white craft paper and provide lots of purple crayons for the children to create their own mural art. Encourage the children to sign their work and share their crayon stories with the rest of the class.

Copy Cat

V

L

T

Y

H

U

O

C

X

A

I Can Write My Name!

Maze

Help the ants find their queen.

Beads

24-35 months
- Strings 3 one-inch beads

36-47 months
- Strings beads on a shoelace

48-59 months
- Strings beads on a shoelace

60+ months
- Strings beads on a shoelace

Beads are fascinating. There are so many different kinds and colors to choose from, no wonder it's a popular activity. While increasing their eye-hand coordination children also learn about patterning and develop dexterity through manipulating beads. Begin with large beads for little hands and as the children mature try smaller and smaller varieties of beads.

Keep your own set of wooden classroom beads. Plan other activities where the children can take their beading projects home. You can do this by providing an assortment of plastic beads or buttons, or by making your own beads from clay, paper, cut straws, or cereal. Stringing beads onto shoelaces is recommended because the ends are already wrapped for pushing through small holes. Dipping the ends of yarn in glue (then letting it dry thoroughly), wrapping the ends of string with tape, or using plastic string will have a similar effect for take-home projects.

Use beads as an incentive for good behavior. Have the children individually (or as a class) collect beads as they follow directions or have good behavior in class. Offer special beads for extra special tasks or behaviors. Let the children take their bead strings home at the end of the week.

[2-3] Bead Bracelets

Use a chenille stem for easy beading activities. The sturdiness of the wire makes it easier for little hands to push buttons or beads over the ends. Twist the ends together and you have an instant bracelet. Use beads with letters and colors and have the child see if he can identify all the colors or letters he used in his bracelet. Have him count the number of beads used.

[4-5] Bead Repeat

Have the children choose two or three colors (or varieties) of beads. Create a pattern as you string the beads by alternating colors. Start with a pattern of two and work your way up to more complex patterns as the children grow.

Extend this activity to a counting project by encouraging the children to add a special bead after four beads have been added to their strand. Have them count by 5's by touching the special beads only.

nOoPpQqRrSsTtUuVvWwXxYyZz

Eating

24-35 months
- Holds a small cup in one hand
- Pours from a small cup
- Brings spoon or fork to mouth, palm facing up

36-47 months
- Holds spoon in fingers with palm up
- Stabs food with a fork
- Serves self at table with little spilling

48-59 months
- Butters bread with a knife
- Uses spoon and fork skillfully
- Can pour from a pitcher

60+ months
- Uses a fork and spoon skillfully

Eating and cooking offer a wide variety of opportunities to increase fine motor skills. From making finger sandwiches to pouring the milk, setting the table to cleaning up, children develop many fine motor skills such as eye-hand coordination, dexterity, and hand strength as they learn important self-help skills.

Some of the food preparation skills that children can easily master include: mixing juice, spreading butter or jam on bread, setting the table, and stirring and measuring ingredients. Read the story of the *Little Red Hen*. Have the children help you stir and knead dough then pinch and roll dough into loaves. Spread butter and sprinkle cheese or cinnamon/sugar on top of the bread when it has finished baking.

Other easy cooking opportunities that use small muscle groups include:

- Spread peanut butter on a tortilla. Then roll the tortilla before eating.
- Make an open-faced sandwich by spreading cream cheese on a rice cake and decorating the face with small finger foods such as a carrot nose, shredded cheese hair, olive eyes, and raisin mouth.
- Shell peanuts.
- Spread cream cheese or other sandwich spread between crackers.
- Make small pizzas by squishing ready-to-bake biscuits flat, spreading pizza sauce, grating and sprinkling cheese on top.
- Decorate cookies by frosting and adding sprinkles in the frosting.
- Practice cutting slices of cheese.
- Use salt and pepper shakers, pour liquids, dip foods, and squeeze bottles of condiments.
- Clean up also offers opportunities to wash and dry dishes and to sort utensils.

Eating (continued)

In addition to the activities and skills listed, here are some fun activities to develop fine motor eating skills.

[2] Up to the Top

Fill a small bucket with water. (You may wish to color the water with food coloring.) Provide a small cup and another container for filling. (Be sure to provide towels for clean up, or do this activity where spills won't create a mess.) Have the child dip the cup into the bucket and then pour it into the second container. Count each cupful as it is poured into the second container. Keep dipping and counting until the second container is completely full.

[3] Squeeze Art

Give each child two slices of bread. Fill a plastic squeeze bottle with fruit jam. (You may have to thin the jam slightly to get it to flow through the tip of the squeeze bottle.) Let the children squeeze and doodle in jam by writing letters or drawing pictures on their bread with the jam. When they're done admiring their work, fold the bread in half and enjoy eating the creations.

[4] Fork It Over

Give each child a small bowl of soft foods such as grapes, cheese cubes, marshmallows, etc., a second bowl, and a fork. Have them stab the contents of the first bowl, one item at a time, and move it to the second bowl as they count each item. Have them report the number of objects in their bowl to you. Then have them stab and count the items back into the first bowl to double check their numbers.

[5] Spoon Race

Place a bowl of eggs (one for each child) on one side of the room, and an empty bowl on the other side of the room. Using a large serving spoon, have the children pick up an egg in the spoon, and carry the egg in the spoon across the room to the empty bowl. Gently place the egg into the second bowl to avoid cracking. Repeat until everyone has had a chance to carry an egg. Once everyone has had an opportunity to carry an egg, give each child a small bowl and a fork and show them how to crack the egg into the bowl. Make sure any stray shells have been removed. Then beat the eggs with your fork. Combine all the eggs together to cook and enjoy your scrambled eggs for a snack. Note that hardboiled eggs will eliminate any danger of sticky raw egg messes and work as well.

Dressing and Self Help Skills

24-35 months

- Can unbutton large buttons
- Undresses and dresses with assistance

36-47 months

- Zips and unzips jacket
- Puts shoes on
- Dresses self with some help (buttons, snaps, and zippers)
- Puts on socks (may have difficulty turning the heel)

48-59 months

- Puts on socks with correct heel placement
- Puts shoes on

60+ months

- Unties an apron (behind self)
- Dresses and undresses without assistance
- Ties shoelaces
- Puts shirt on correctly

Dressing is an every day task that children take great pride in mastering. It takes a lot of coordination. The best way to help children develop these skills is to be patient and let them do as much as they can on their own. Young children will need a little assistance, but as they near three years and beyond, children should be able to dress themselves without assistance. In the classroom you can provide additional opportunities for learning dressing and self-help skills through the dress-up center. Provide clothes that require snaps, buttons, or Velcro™ enclosures to be manipulated, shirts to pull on, and pants and dresses to be zippered.

Use the button face file folder game (pp. 34-35) to practice buttoning skills. Incorporate the fun dressing games below to work on dressing and self-help skills.

[2-3] Sock Match

Gather an assortment of colored socks. Make sure that each pair of socks is distinct from every other pair. Place one sock from each pair in a large basket. Give each child one of the matching socks. Have them pull on their sock and then sort through the basket for the sock that matches the sock on their foot. Have each child tell you what makes his socks match.

Extend the activity by playing again, this time instructing the children to choose a sock that does not match the one he is wearing. Have him explain what is different and similar about the two mismatched socks.

[3-4] Lacing

Punch holes around the outside edge of a paper plate. Using yarn or curling ribbon, string the yarn through the holes. Practice going back and forth across the circle to the next hole, and also lacing through each hole around the edge.

Extend the activity by randomly numbering the holes around the plate. Have the children lace through each numbered hole sequentially.

Button Face File Folder Game

- Make a copy of both button face file folder pattern pages (34–35).
- Use the shapes on this page as a template for cutting the facial features from felt. Make a slit through each piece where indicated on the pattern.
- Color the button face as desired, paste it to the inside of a file folder, and laminate for durability. Using large $1\frac{1}{2}$" buttons, quilting thread, and a sharp needle, sew the buttons to the button face where indicated with an "x." Leave a little slack in the thread so the buttons are tight, but still have a little "give" to them.
- Staple a small zippered bag to the inside of the file folder and place the felt face features inside.
- To Play: Slide the felt face features over the buttons on the head to create a funny button face.

Button Face

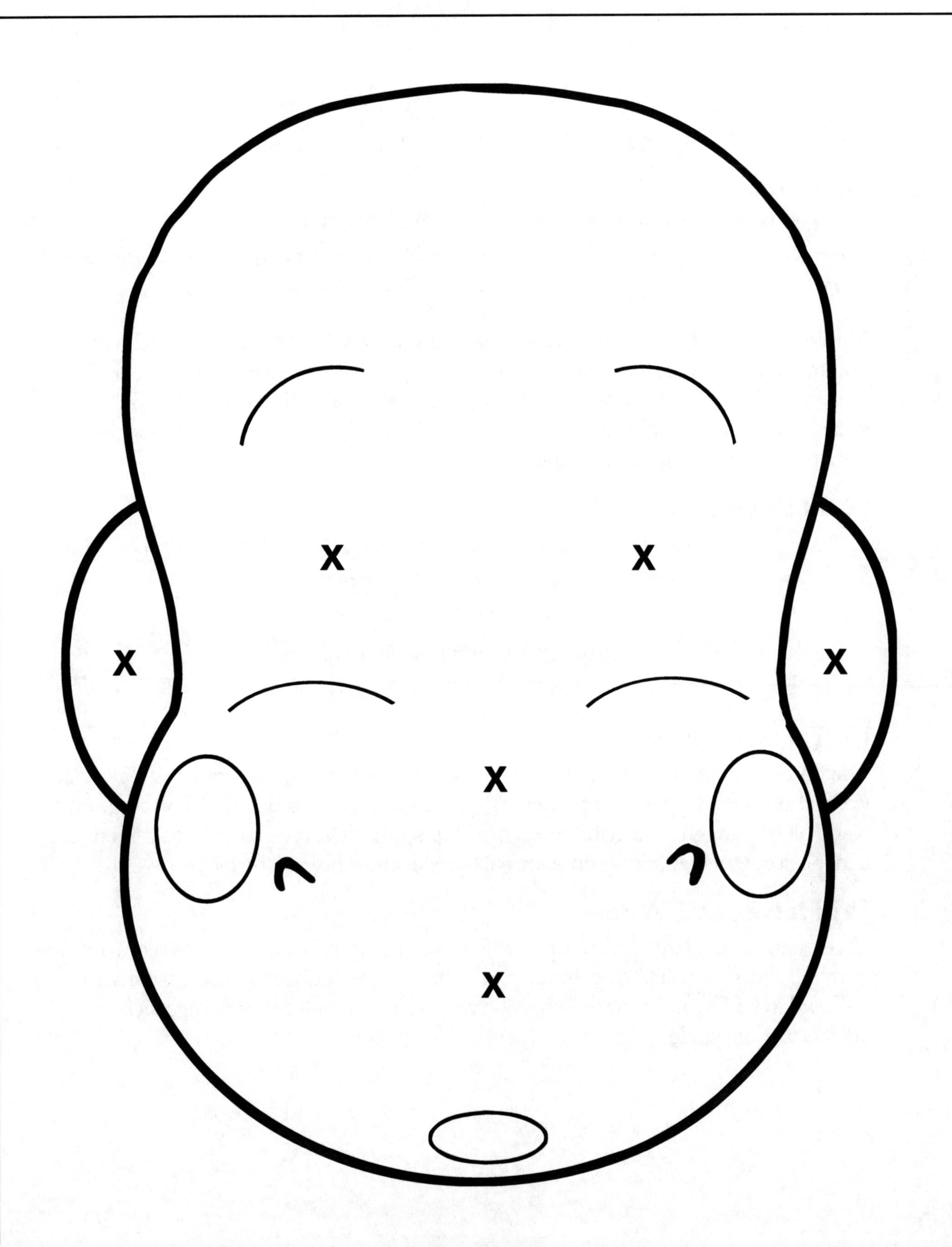

Play Dough

24-35 months

- Rolls, pounds, squeezes, and pulls clay

36-47 months

- Manipulates clay (rolls balls, snakes, uses cookie cutters)

48-59 months

- Manipulates clay to create animal and human forms

60+ months

- Manipulates clay to create animal and human forms

Manipulating clay and dough is not only a great way to extend fine motor skills and muscle strength, it is also a very soothing activity. Children can roll, push, pull, pound, cut, and squish to help express emotions and frustrations. But playing with dough is only half the fun. Let the children help you mix and create the dough for added fine motor experiences.

[2-5] Dough Song

(Sing to the tune of "Row, Row, Row Your Boat.")

Push, push, push and pull
Tug and pat and pound.
Push and pull and pinch and pound,
Roll it 'round and 'round!

[3-5] Hall of Fame

Start a clay creation "Hall of Fame." After creating your masterpieces, bake or leave the dough to dry. Paint them as desired, name your dough creation, and place all the dough on a windowsill or table so that everyone can enjoy each other's creations. At circle time let each child share his masterpiece.

[5] Halves and Wholes

Give each child a large ball of dough. Press or roll it into a circle. Ask him to divide it in half with a small plastic knife. Have the children continue cutting pieces in half and in half again. Now see if you can put all the halves back together to create one big circle.

Play Dough (continued)

[3] Counting Balls

On pieces of construction paper write the numbers 1–10 in large script, one number per page. Across the bottom of each page, draw 1" circles to represent the number written on the page. Color the circles. Laminate for durability.

To play, have the children choose a card and make the number of dough balls indicated on the paper. Place them on the colored circles on the page.

Extend the activity by creating laminated cards that have spirals, swirls, wavy lines, and letters. Have the children roll snakes out of the dough and then form them to match the lines on their card.

[4] Play Dough Sharing

Make three batches of play dough. Color one batch red, another yellow, and the third blue. Divide the dough so that each child has one ball of red, yellow, or blue dough. Have the children experiment with mixing colors by "sharing" with a child who has a color that is different from his own. Each child pulls a small bit from their ball and shares it by mixing it with another child. Now divide this new color in two so that both have some of the new color. Repeat with other children.

Cooked Modeling Dough

2 c. flour
1 c. salt
2 c. water
3 T. alum (pickling spice)
2 T. vegetable oil
Color and spices for scent (optional)

Mix flour, salt, and alum in a heavy cooking pan. Add water, cooking oil, and colors or scents as desired. Stir over low heat until mixture gels and pulls away from the pan. Knead immediately and store in an air-tight container.

Salt Dough

1 c. flour
$\frac{1}{2}$ ***c. salt***
$\frac{1}{2}$ ***c. water***
$\frac{1}{4}$ ***c. vegetable oil***

Mix flour and salt. Add the water and vegetable oil slowly while stirring. Add water a few drops at a time if the dough is too dry, or add flour by the teaspoonful if too sticky. Knead well. Bake at 225° for 2 hours to harden if desired.

AaBbCcDdEeFfGgHhIiJjKkLlMm

Motor Skills

Puzzles

24-35 months
- Completes a three-piece puzzle

36-47 months
- Completes a 5–6 piece puzzle

48-59 months
- Completes a 7–10 piece puzzle

60+ months
- Completes a 10–15 piece puzzle

Puzzles are a fantastic activity for developing eye-hand coordination and dexterity. Puzzles also develop skills in spatial awareness, shapes, and orientation. For very young preschoolers, simple 3–4 piece puzzles help begin their puzzling skills and give them success before they can get frustrated. As children mature, puzzles with more pieces and more complex-shaped pieces can be used.

Help children learn to be puzzle detectives by helping them see that they can look for clues as they are assembling their puzzle. Start by looking for similar features or colors. Ask questions such as, "Does this piece look like it might be part of the barn or part of a tree?" Look for colors or patterns on the edges of pieces to match them up with the next piece. Finally, help them see the shapes of the connecting pieces. Little tabs aren't going to fit well in big holes and vice versa.

Make your own puzzles out of photographs of the children, or by using posters, or the children's artwork. (Be certain you get permission before cutting a work of art into puzzle pieces!)

Use the File Folder Puzzles to create activities for each age level (pages 39–42). Make a copy of each pattern page. Color as desired. Carefully cut out each figure leaving the frame intact. Carefully separate the remaining pieces where indicated with dotted lines. Mount the frame on one side of a file folder. Laminate the puzzle frame and the separated pieces. Trim the puzzle pieces flush with the edge. Place the puzzle pieces in a zippered bag that has been stapled to the file folder.

A

B C

File Folder Puzzle—2 Year

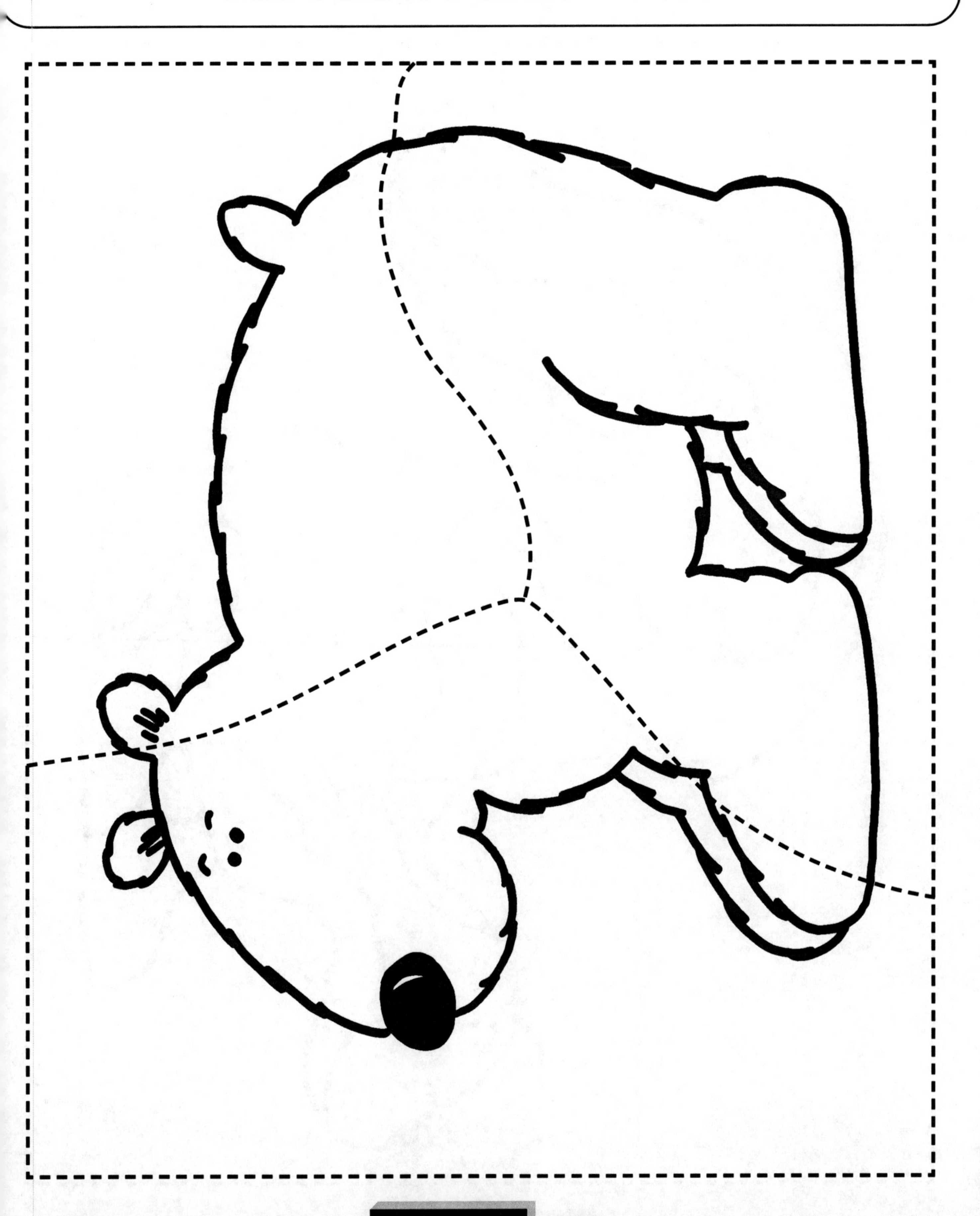

File Folder Puzzle—3 Year

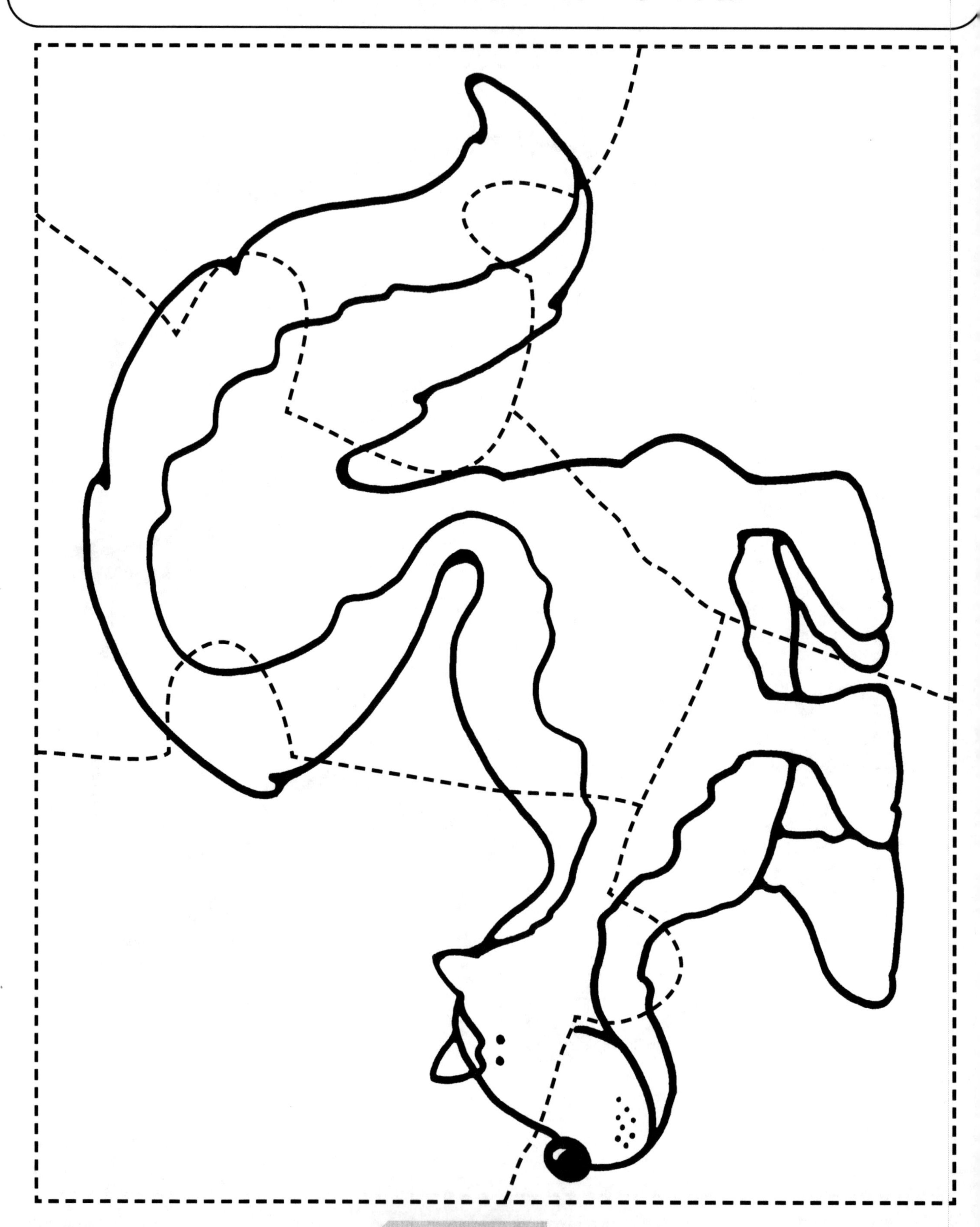

File Folder Puzzle—4 Year

File Folder Puzzle—5 Year

Gross Motor Activities

Strengthening muscles, gaining balance and coordination, and improving eye-hand coordination are just a few of the skills children learn every day doing the things they love to do. And what do they love to do? Children love to play with ride-on toys, jungle gyms, swings, slides, hoops, balls, trikes, and other playground equipment. They love somersaulting, skipping, playing tag, following the leader, and moving to music. Gross motor activities rarely need encouragement or direction. Sometimes it seems as though children's bodies were meant to be in motion all the time. In addition to the other activities that highlight specific gross motor activities in the pages that follow, here are a few any-time favorites.

Balloon Fun

Start with several different sizes and kinds of inflated balloons. Have the children choose one balloon, and see if they can 'bop' another balloon around the play area by hitting it with their balloon. Play balloon baseball or balloon golf by hitting a small round balloon with a long twisting balloon.

Tie the neck of a balloon to a string, and the strings to their legs and arms. Encourage them to run as fast as they can and imagine the balloon taking them high in the air as they watch them float and dance behind them. See how many ways they can make their balloons move.

Fill a very large bucket with water balloons. Draw a face or target on a sheet of poster board with washable markers. Let the children toss water balloons until the color is washed off the poster.

Fill a wading pool with water and see if you can sink a balloon filled with air by hitting it with balloons filled with water.

Horseback Riding

If you don't have the real thing, or even the next best thing (a stick horse), saddle up a pool "noodle" for some fancy riding. Have the children name their horse and take their favorite pal for a spin. Have them take their horse out in the arena (playground) and let them maneuver around barrels or buckets or open up into a full gallop.

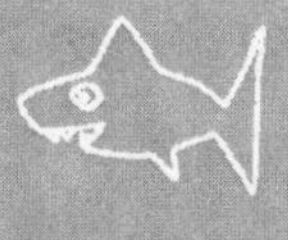

Gross Motor Activities (continued)

Footprint Walk

Make several copies of the Footprints page (p. 55). Lay each footprint type out in a straight line across the play area. Designate each set of footprints as a different animal walk. For example set 1 will be regular walking, set 2 will be bear crawling, set 3 hopping like a bird, and set 4 will be a horse galloping. Divide the class up into 4 teams. Have each team line up behind one set of footprint cards. At your signal, have the first children in each line follow the footprint path in front of them as directed. Once they reach the end of the footprints have them return in reverse to the starting point. When everyone in the team has finished the walk, swap places with another team and try the new footprint path. Change the activities for each footprint path and play again.

Training Camp

Football players have to work hard to get in shape to play. Here are some fun activities to include in your own "preschool training camp."

- Set rings or tires in a row and have the children jump from one ring to the next.
- Toss footballs at a target or through a hoop hung from a tree branch.
- Do calisthenics such as push-ups, sit-ups, jumping jacks, or lift sticks or blocks for weights.
- Run around the building while chanting or singing.
- Tackle large pillows or blow-up animals.

Tin Can Bowling

Gather an assortment of aluminum or tin cans. Decorate as desired. Stack the cans in a pyramid. Draw or tape a line about ten feet from the cans and have the children experiment to find which ball is best to bowl into the cans. Have the children count the number of cans they knock over.

Beach Ball Blowout

Gather a beach ball for each child to play with. Have them lie on their backs with the ball between their legs. See if they can raise and lower their legs and hang on to the ball at the same time. Now have them switch the ball into their hands and bring the ball back over their heads to the ground and then straight up in the air above their heads again.

Gross Motor Activities (continued)

Blanket Fun

Using a parachute or a large blanket, see how high, low, fast, or slow you can bop a small stuffed animal. Add a few other soft objects such as ping-pong balls or socks. Partner the children into pairs. Have each child hold the ends of a large towel, and let them try tossing and catching balls, beanbags, or stuffed animals with their mini-parachute.

Bowling For Kids

Select three or four children to help you bowl. Form a "circle" around the rest of the children. Have the rest of the class gather together in the middle of the children you have selected to be "bowlers." Roll or toss a large beach ball into the crowd of children. When a child gets hit with the ball they then come to the outside circle and help you bowl for other children. Continue playing until there are only one or two children left. Have them come to the outer circle to be the new tossers.

Bumper Cars

Purchase inexpensive blow-up pool rings, one for each child. Have each child slip an inflated ring over his head so that it rests around the child's tummy. Have the children hold onto their rings with their arms. Designate a safe playing area where with lots of space to run. While holding onto their rings, show the children how to gently bump into another child's ring. As they bounce off, they can find another friend to bump and bounce with.

Scoops and Buckets

Scatter a variety of objects throughout the playing area. Suggested items might include: straws, ping-pong balls, plastic practice golf balls, socks, small toys, milk jug lids, paper cups, plastic spoons, etc. Label a bucket or box for each child and place them along the wall on one side of the room. Give each child a scoop. (You can make one by cutting the sides off a plastic milk jug.) Instruct the children that you want them to gather as many objects as they can before you signal to stop. The children then should pick up an item with the scoop, walk to their buckets, and empty their scoop before returning for a second item. Continue playing for a few minutes or until all the items are collected.

Have each child find a spot on the floor where he can empty his bucket without getting the contents mixed up with a neighbor. Have the children sort the contents of their buckets into piles. Have the children count how many of each item and then share the total number of the item they have. Using the items they collected see if they can create simple patterns (spoon, ball, spoon, ball).

AaBbCcDdEeFfGgHhIiJjKkLlMn

Motor Skills

Balls

24-35 months

- Throws a small ball underhand 5–7 ft.
- Kicks ball forward
- Catches a ball with straight arms in front of body

36-47 months

- Catches a ball
- Throws overhead
- Kicks a ball forward
- Kicks a rolling ball
- Throws a ball underhand 9'
- Catches a bounced ball

48-59 months

- Throws overhand
- Catches a large thrown ball
- Kicks ball forward
- Catches a bounced ball most of the time

60+ months

- Catches bounced balls
- Throws balls overhead
- Catches a thrown ball

Playing with balls is a great way to move large muscle groups. Catching, throwing, and kicking balls require coordination, balance, and muscle control. Start with large balls for very young children and use incrementally smaller balls as the developmental age grows older. Keep a large assortment of balls on hand for play including tennis, beach, rubber playground, ping-pong, soccer, football, etc. Having an assortment will mean that you'll have enough for everyone, and the game will always be a little different, a little more challenging with each new ball that is introduced.

Yarn Balls

Create your own soft balls for indoor play out of yarn. Cut a 4 x 4 square of cardboard. Tape a 6" strand of yarn down the middle of the cardboard. Tape the end of a skein of yarn to the board so that it lies perpendicular across the first string. Wrap the yarn around the cardboard form 50–75 times (the more times you wrap, the fuller the ball will be). Loosen the 6" strand and tie it securely around all the wrapped yarn loops. Turn the cardboard over and cut the yarn down the middle. Trim off overhanging strands and fluff the yarn into a ball.

Balls (continued)

Sponge Balls

Cut several soft foam sponges into 1" strips. (The size of your ball will depend on the length of sponge you use.) Gather ten strips together, matching ends. Connect through the middle of the sponge strips with a twist tie or plastic tie-back cord.

[2-5] Bucket Bounce

Gather six large buckets. Fill each one with water. Draw a line on the sidewalk with chalk to mark a starting point. Place the first bucket 2' from the starting line, the second 3' and so on until the final bucket is in line. Have a child line up at the starting line and toss a tennis ball into the first bucket. Retrieve the ball and try tossing the ball into the second bucket. Continue playing until the ball goes into all five buckets.

To extend the game, move the buckets back as the child successfully hits the last one.

[2-5] Catch and Go

Use balls and catching skills as a transition from one activity to the next. Using soft plastic balls, tape a message such as "I love you" or "Gimmie five!" on the side of each ball. As you transition to line up, toss a ball to a child who is sitting quietly and is ready to line up. Have them remove the note and bring it to you for reading. Be sure everyone leaves the circle with a hug, handshake, wink, or smile from you.

[3] In, Over, Under, Around, and Through

Set up a ball obstacle course that requires throwing a ball into a basket, bouncing it over a swing seat or other obstacle, rolling it under a friend's legs, kicking it around a tree, and throwing it through a hoop. Try the obstacle course with several different balls. Which ball was the best for throwing? Which was the easiest to kick? Which ball was the best all around?

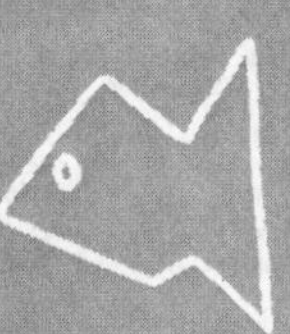

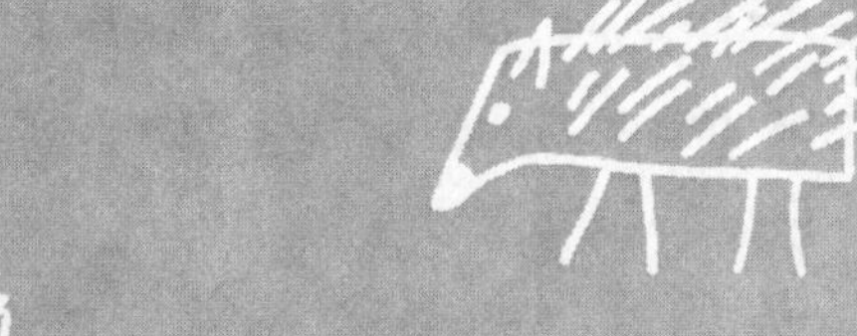
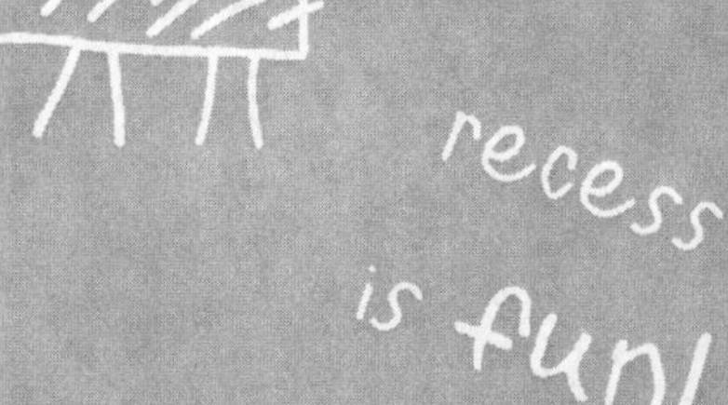

1-57029-529-8 *Solutions Series: Gross & Fine Motor Skills*

Balls (continued)

[3] Hit and Run

This is a fun game that can be played solo or in pairs. To play by yourself, choose a ping-pong ball and paddle. Throw or hold the ball in the air and swat it away with the paddle. Chase after it and hit from where the ball landed. To play with a partner, switch off hitting as you both run together from place to place around the playground.

[3-5] Buddy Bounce

Divide the class into small groups of six children. Have these groups stand in a circle. Hand one child a ball and instruct him to choose a buddy. Have him say one nice thing about this child and then bounce the ball to the child he called out. After everyone in the circle has been complimented and buddy-bounced, mix up the circles and start again.

[3-5] Alphabet Pass

Have the whole class stand in a wide circle. Tell the class that you're going to be tossing and catching the alphabet. Hand the ball to the first child and have her say "A." She then tosses it to the next child in the circle who then says "B." Continue tossing and alphabetizing until you get to the end of the alphabet.

Extend the activity to other skills such as rhyming words or matching beginning sounds as you toss the ball from friend to friend.

[4-5] Wall Ball

Gather an assortment of bouncy balls. Mark a line about four feet away from a solid wall. Have the children toss the balls against the wall and see if they can catch it on the rebound. Continue tossing and catching. Then try kicking the ball. Move back if catching gets too easy. What happens if you throw or kick hard? Can you kick the ball soft enough to get very close to the wall without touching it?

[4-5] Bounce Spots

Cut several circles out of a rubber bath mat. Place the rubber circles randomly around the playground. Using a bouncing ball, bounce the ball (using two hands) around the playground and on each spot.

To extend the activity, write numbers on the spots and have the children bounce the spots in numerical order.

Balancing

24-35 months

- Walks 2–3 steps on a balance beam
- Balances on one foot for several seconds

36-47 months

- Stands on one foot for two or more seconds
- Bends over without falling

48-59 months

- Stands on one foot eight seconds
- Touches toes without bending knees

60+ months

- Balances on either foot for ten seconds
- Stands on one foot with eyes closed without loosing balance
- Bends and touches toes without bending knees

Balance is one of those skills that effect many other skills. Walking, running, tip-toeing, and jumping all tax a child's ability to balance himself. Obviously the balance beam is a great tool for exercising balancing skills. You may also want to consider incorporating some yoga and tai chi movements into your balancing and stretching activities.

[2-5] Bend and Touch Action Rhyme

Reach high, reach low (*reach hands overhead then swing them down to the floor*)

Run fast, run slow (*run in place fast, then slow*)

Arms out then touch your toes (*reach arms out wide then bend over to touch toes*)

Reach forward, reach back (*reach hands in front and then in back of you*)

Let your back go slack (*relax and bend forward at the waist*)

Can you touch your knee to your nose? (*try to touch knee with nose*)

Reach left, reach right (*reach left, reach right*)

Reach up into the night (*reach up into the air*)

Then tickle your little toes (*bend down and tickle toes*)

Do the actions while repeating the rhyme. Then repeat it while standing on one leg, and then the other.

Balancing (continued)

[2-5] Flamingo Tag

Flamingos stand on one leg, tucking the other up underneath their bodies. Have everyone pretend to be like flamingos by standing on one leg with their wings (arms) tucked under their bodies. Now have the children spread out over the playing area, so there is room to move between each child. Choose one child to be "it." At your signal, all the children begin running around the play area, trying to avoid getting tagged. When tagged, the child then turns into a flamingo and stands on one leg like a flamingo. Continue playing until everyone turns into a flamingo (children can switch legs if one gets tired). Choose a new person to be it and play again.

[3] I'm a Little Tea Pot

Sing:

I'm a little teapot,
Short and stout.
Here is my handle, (*place hand on hip*)
Here is my spout. (*hold other arm out to the side*)
When I get all steamed up
Hear me shout:
"Tip me over and pour me out!" (*tip to the side and see how far you can go without falling over*)

[4-5] Troll Under the Bridge

Use a balance beam for a bridge. Select one child to be the troll under the bridge. Have the rest of the children line up at one end of the balance beam. As the first person approaches the balance beam the troll calls out "Who's that tramping over my bridge?" The child in line then announces his name and requests permission to pass over the bridge. The troll obliges, but the child must first perform a feat of skill before crossing over such as counting backwards from 10 or counting to 50 by 5s.

Trike-Riding

24-35 months
- Steers and pedals a tricycle

36-47 months
- Rides a trike

48-59 months
- Rides a trike skillfully

60+ months
- Rides a trike skillfully, perhaps maneuvering obstacles

Tricycle riding is a hallmark skill for preschoolers. Regardless of the age of the children you are teaching, it is bound to be a popular activity. Young preschoolers will find pedaling a big challenge. But once they gain the coordination necessary to keep the trike moving forward, they're off and running.

[2-5] Stop Then Go

Create the stop/go traffic sign as directed (pp. 56–57). Choose one child to be the traffic officer. As the children pedal around the playground, she can stop them at any time by holding up the "stop" sign and then signaling forward again by holding up the "go" sign. Switch riders after a few minutes and choose a new traffic officer.

[3-5] Obstacle Course

Create a tricycle obstacle course by using ramps, bumps (riding over a hose for example), around cones, under archways, etc. Use the Activity Flags (p. 54) to suggest activities to stop and do along the way. For example, pedal around the cones and stop at Flag #1. Get off your trike and do 10 jumping jacks. Get back on the trike and ride under the streamers hanging from the tree branch and stop at flag #2. Have the children pedal as fast as they can safely go and time their laps.

[4-5] Tricycle Memory Game

Tape pictures of familiar preschool objects such as animals, a crayon, a shoe, a house, an egg, etc., around the playground. Have the children pedal around a course that takes them past all the pictures. When they return from their ride ask the riders how many pictures they saw. Have children try to remember each one. Send them around again to see if they can find something they missed before.

Running and Walking

24-35 months
- Walks backwards ten or more feet
- Runs forward well

36-47 months
- Runs easily
- Walks a straight line
- Walks smoothly forward, backward, or sideways

48-59 months
- Runs around obstacles
- Walks backward toe-to-heel
- Moves forward and backward with agility

60+ months
- Run, gallops, and tumbles
- Walks backward, toe touching heel

It's as easy as getting from here to there, but from the first awkward steps to running with agility, walking is a skill that continues to grow gradually throughout the preschool years. In addition to walking everywhere, there are lots of fun activities you can do with your children to continue to strengthen the leg muscles, enhance coordination, and balance as your children gain control over these large muscle groups. Of course allowing for lots of time to run and play on the playground will increase these skills, too. Tag and other running games are always popular activities. Here are a few other ideas to get you started.

[2-5] Yarn Paths
Using brightly colored yarn, tape a path along the floor. Use tape where needed to create wavy, straight, zig-zagged, and curly lines. Have the children walk each line heel-to-toe from the beginning to the end. Now try each maze in reverse.

Extend this activity by placing two straight paths next to one another so that the yarn paths are about 12" apart. Have the children first walk along the lines individually. Next, have them place one foot on one line, and the other foot on the second line and walk from one end to the next. Move the second line another few inches away from the first and try the two-foot walk again.

[3-5] Yarn Maps
Use different colored yarn to create colored paths to different centers or activities in the room. Place paths from each activity to each of the other activities.

Running and Walking (continued)

[2-5] Follow Me Footprints

Make several copies of the footprints (p.55) on colored paper. Separate along the dotted lines and laminate for durability. Create footprint trails by placing copies of the same footprints in a line that weaves to another part of the playground. Make a separate trail for each different set of footprints. On the first trail, put the footsteps quite close together. On the second trail separate the footprint markers by a few inches. Repeat with the third and fourth trails making each on successively more spread apart. Encourage the children to try each trail forwards and backwards.

[4-5] Walk and Stop

Trace a long path around the sidewalk with chalk. Create several Activity Flags (p.54) and place them along the path to give suggested activities to stop and perform. Once a child reaches a flag he stops, does the activity and then continues on the yarn path to the next sign and activity.

[3-5] Stop and Go

Assemble a two-sided stop and go sign (see Stop and Go Signs pp. 56–57). Line all the children up on one side of the playground. Choose one child to be "it." Have this child flash the "go" side of the sign when he wants the children to walk forward and the "stop" side of the sign when he wants them to stop. Continue flashing the stop and go sign until someone reaches the other side. Vary the walking by suggesting baby steps, tippy-toe walking, etc.

[4-5] Backwards Obstacle Course

Create an obstacle course with things to jump over, walk around, and climb under. The catch is that the entire course must be done in reverse. All walking, crawling, and jumping must be done backwards.

[4-5] Directing Traffic

Line all the children up so they have some room to move about in front, behind and to the sides of one another. Make sure everyone can see you. (You may want to wear large, brightly colored gloves to get and keep the children's attention). Tell them that every time you blow a whistle you will want them to walk in the direction you indicate. If you signal forward, they should walk forward. If you signal to the left, they should shuffle sideways to the left, etc. Hold up the stop sign (p. 56) when you want the children to stop. Blow the whistle again as you signal the new direction to go. Increase the speed of your signals as the children get the hang of it.

Activity Flags Pattern

Make as many copies of this page as desired on colored copy paper. Cut and laminate for durability. Write directions on the flags as directed in your activity. Tape the flag to a stick or wooden skewer. Fill a plastic food container with gravel and seal tight with a lid. Make a small hole in the lid and insert the flag. Place the flags as markers in your obstacle courses or other games as directed.

1. **Do 10 jumping jacks.**

2. **Hop up and down 8 times.**

3. **Count out loud, 1-10.**

4. **Touch your toes 10 times.**

5. **Clap your hands 12 times.**

6. **Circle the flag 5 times.**

Footprints

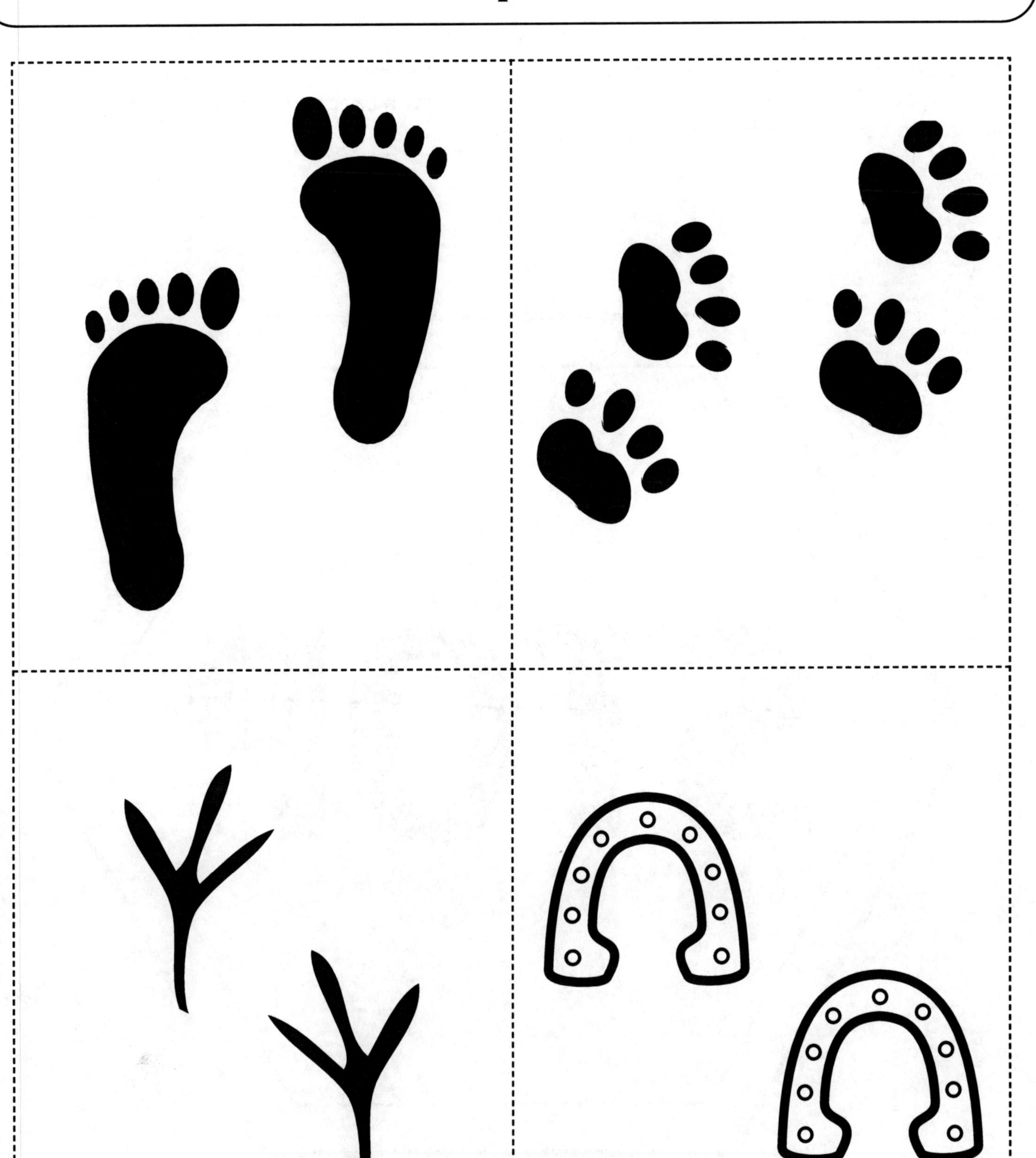

Stop

Make a copy of this page on red copy paper. Laminate and mount to a large dowel or paint stirring stick. Make a copy of the "Go" sign (p. 57) on green paper and mount to the opposite side of the dowel or stick to create a stop/go sign.

Go

Make a copy of this page on green copy paper. Laminate and mount to a large dowel or paint stirring stick. Make a copy of the "Stop" sign (p. 56) on red paper and mount to the opposite side of the dowel or stick to create a stop/go sign.

AaBbCcDdEeFfGgHhIiJjKkLlMm

Motor Skills

Tiptoes

24-35 months

- Walks on tiptoes a few seconds

36-47 months

- Stands on tiptoes a few seconds
- Walks a short distance on tiptoes

48-59 months

- Walks a short distance on tiptoes
- Balances on tiptoes for 10 or more seconds

60+ months

- Balances on tiptoes for 10 or more seconds
- Runs on tiptoes a few seconds

Tiptoeing is an important preschool skill because it combines balance with walking. It increases muscle strength in the feet and calves and gives a child's brain a whole new orientation for walking. Using tiptoeing in your transitions will keep feet quiet and attention focused on one thing—walking. Sneak into the next activity or to the gym and practice good behavior and gross motor skills at the same time!

[2-5] Tiptoe Tutus

Create colorful tutus by taping colored paper streamers to a 3' length of curling ribbon. Tie the tutus around each child's waist. Play some ballet or dancing music and have children tiptoe around in tutus to the music.

[2-5] Tiptoe Through the Tulips

Make several copies of the footprints on page 55. Make several copies of a tulip-shaped flower (see illustration below) out of colored construction paper. Tape all the footprints randomly around the floor, making certain that each footprint is accessible from another footprint in one tiptoe step. Fill in the spaces around the footprints with the tulips. Have each child choose a footprint to stand on. Instruct them to step only on the footprints, not on the tulips. At your signal everyone begins tiptoeing across the tulip field. If a child happens to miss a footprint and steps on a tulip instead, have her join you on the side until several children are "out." Begin the game again.

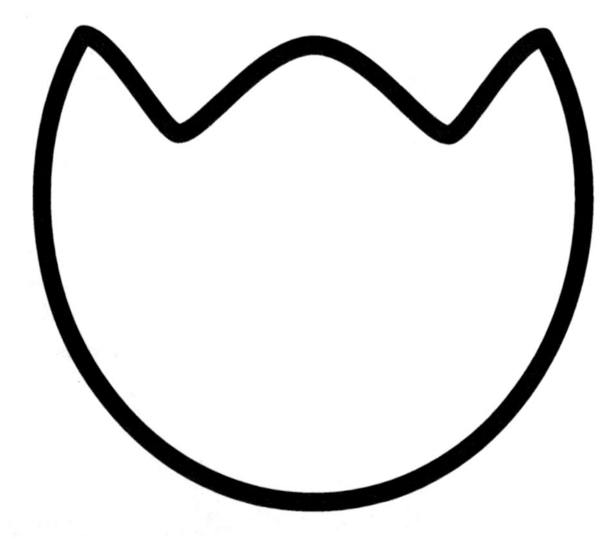

Tiptoes (continued)

[3-5] Sneaking Game

Have one child sit at the front of the classroom. Have her turn her back to the rest of the class. Have all the others sit quietly on the floor. Tell them you will be tapping one of them on the head and they must then sneak up on tiptoes to the child who is sitting at the front of the class. If she hears them she turns around and that child must return to his seat. If the child successfully sneaks up on the child who is "it," he swaps places with her and a new game begins.

[3-5] Tiptoe Races

This race measures not how fast, but how far each child can tiptoe. Start the first child from a given point. Have her tiptoe as far as she can go. Using a measuring tape, mark the distance the first child tiptoed and write it down on a poster board next to her name. Repeat with all the other children in the class writing each of their distances down on the poster. After everyone has had a chance to tiptoe, add up all the children's tiptoe efforts to see how far the class tiptoed all together. Compare that distance with other familiar distances, such as: We tiptoed the entire length of an apatosaurus, or We tiptoed around our school 7 times!

Repeat the activity, this time having the children count the number of steps they take. Add up all the tiptoe steps for a class total. Repeat again seeing if the children can tiptoe with giant or baby steps. Which way is easier and why?

[4-5] Tiptoe Tag

Have the children play tag while pretending to tiptoe through hot lava. Have one child be "it" and chase the other children around. Have a few "safe spots" designated that the children can tiptoe to, to keep their feet from getting too toasty (or their legs too tired). If they are in the "safe spot" they can only stay while they count to 10. Then they must tiptoe off again.

Add two or three children to be "it" for a faster-paced game.

AaBbCcDdEeFfGgHhIiJjKkLlMm

Motor Skills

Pushing and Pulling

24-35 months

- Pulls wheeled toys by a string

36-47 months

- Pushes and pulls wheeled toys

48-59 months

- Moves large objects by pushing and pulling

60+ months

- Moves large objects by pushing and pulling

From the very first efforts of pulling toys around on a string, to the more complex movements of moving large objects, pushing and pulling skills involve arms, legs, and back muscles. As children grow, they can adapt their play to include more complex thought patterns so pushing a toy truck turns into "How can I push this truck up the slide?" or "How can I get this heavy box across the room?" In addition to flexing those growing muscles, pushing and pulling activities give children an opportunity to explore properties of physics, and scientific concepts such as friction and gravity.

[2-3] Make-It-Yourself Toys

While there are many pushing and pulling toys that are commercially available, you can turn any wheeled toy into a pushing or pulling toy by attaching string or a long dowel. Find several cars or trucks and attach a string to the front bumper. Have the children pull the toys around obstacles in the classroom or on the playground. Create a ramp by propping a large board up on boxes or bricks. Have the children pull their toys up and over the hills. Talk about which is easier, up or down, and why. Have them try to push or pull the toys up the steps. Does it work? Why or why not? Load the back of a truck up with heavy blocks. Did this make a difference in how you were able to pull the truck? Encourage the children to explore new ways of pushing and pulling their toys.

[2-5] Pull Me

Children love to go on "rides." Showing them how they can safely push and pull one another around will give the children opportunities to flex their muscles and interact with one another.

Tie a sturdy rope to the front of a large laundry basket. Have one child sit inside the basket while a friend pulls him around the room. (This works best on indoor surfaces.) If an extra hand is needed, another child can push from behind.

Boxes are another source of pushing and pulling fun. Attach a rope to one side and pull, or push from behind. Have box races by having two teams push a box from one end of the room or play area to the other. Set up an obstacle course to maneuver your boxes around.

nOoPpQqRrSsTtUuVvWwXxYyZz

Pushing and Pulling (continued)

[2-5] Wagon Train

Wagons are fun toys for increasing pushing and pulling skills. Fill a wagon with toys (or a friend) and go for a spin. Fill a wagon with several balls. Try pulling the wagon around the playground without loosing any toys over the side. If your wagon will hold water, fill it with water and see how far you can go without spilling.

Lay a long (12–24') sheet of dark craft paper along the sidewalk. Roll the wagon through a puddle of water and then pull it along the paper path. See the wagon wheel prints left behind. Let them evaporate and let a friend try.

[4-5] Paper Pusher

Try this fun game, using arms only for pushing. Wad up a sheet of newspaper. Place it on the ground and push it as far as you can with your arms. Crawl forward and push again. Continue crawling and pushing until you reach the other side of the room or playground.

Try it again using only your feet, nose, head, or other part of your body for pushing practice.

[4-5] Pushing Problem

Fill a box with several heavy blocks. Have the children work together as partners to see if they can figure out how to move the blocks from one side of the room to the other. They may need to rest it on a blanket and pull it over, get more help from friends, take two trips, or load the box into something with wheels and then replace the blocks to move it.

Try moving the box by balancing it on your own created "wheels." Place a couple of playground balls under the box. Push the box forward. As the box moves forward, place another ball in front of the box and pick up the ball that you just rolled the box off and bring it to the front of the box. Continue rolling over the balls to reach your final destination. How many other ways can you move your box?

Stairs

24-35 months

- Climbs stairs (two feet to each step)

36-47 months

- Walks downstairs one foot on each step

48-59 months

- Goes upstairs and downstairs without support

60+ months

- Walks down the stairs, alternating feet

Learning to climb stairs takes a lot of muscle strength, balance, and coordination. It takes lots of patience to wait for little feet to navigate the stairs one at a time. But practice and experience is what will help children gain confidence and skills in stair climbing.

[2-3] Stair Surprises

Place a small item at the top of a flight of stairs (you may have to hide it inside a paper bag if you want to keep it a surprise until everyone reaches the top stair). Sing the "Stair Climbing Song" below as you climb the stairs and find the surprise.

Stair Climbing Song

(*Sing to the tune of "The Bear Went Over the Mountain."*)

Oh, we're going up the stairs,
We're going up the stairs,
We're going up the stairs,
To see what we can see (*look for the surprise*).
And all that we can see,
And all that we can see,
Is a ________ at the top of the stairs,
A ________ at the top of the stairs,
A ________ at the top of the stairs
Is all that we can see!

[4-5] Bounce Up, Bounce Down

Use a large rubber ball. Bounce and catch the ball on the next stair up as you repeat the following action rhyme.

One step, two step, three step bop.
Don't give up 'til you're at the top.
Four step, five step, six step bop,
Up, and up, and up, don't stop!

Jumping

24-35 months

- Jumps in place two or more times
- Jumps backwards
- Jumps forward on both feet 8–14 inches

36-47 months

- Jumps over a 6" barrier with both feet
- Jumps off an 18" object with one foot leading
- Jumps off a 2' object with both feet and lands with both feet
- Jump ropes two cycles
- Hops in place on one foot

48-59 months

- Hops forward on one foot three or more times
- Jumps forward 10 times without falling over
- Hops on one foot up to five seconds

60+ months

- Jump ropes
- Jumps over knee-high obstacles
- Hops forward on one foot five or more times

With all the hopping and jumping on, over, and around that children do, it's amazing they don't learn to jump before they learn to walk. Developing the muscle strength and coordination to lift yourself off the ground is an exhilarating experience for chronic jumpers. Practice jumping high, low, fast, slow, forward, backward, and sideways. Play some favorite music and hop on one leg or jump while holding hands with a partner. Use the activity flags (p. 54), the footprints (p. 55) and the stop and go sign (pp. 56–57) to set up a jumping obstacle course.

Start jumping through a hula hoop by swinging it up over your head and then jumping over the hoop as it passes under your feet to begin with. Graduate to a real jump rope once you've got the hang of it. Now that you're warmed up with all this jumping, try these fun activities until you're all jumped out.

[2] Hop to It

Have a child visually locate an object across the room. On your command, have him hop or jump across the room to retrieve the object and return with it by jumping back to you.

Extend the activity by letting the child decide what to bring you. Give him one-dimensional clues such as, "Bring me something red." As he masters this skill, give him two clues such as, "Bring me something that is red and big."

Jumping (continued)

[3] Lily Pad Leap Frog

Cut several large lily pad shapes out of green craft paper. Make sure there is one for each child in the class. Tape these securely to the floor in a random order. Let the children take turns hopping from one pad to the next.

Extend the activity by taping the lily pads in a circle. Choose one child to start and instruct him to hop over the children in front of him all the way around the circle until he reaches his own lily pad home. Have the next child in line leap frog over his classmates and then continue on around the circle until everyone has had a chance to leap over all the other little frogs.

[3-5] Kangaroo Tag

Just as it sounds, this game of tag involves a lot of jumping. Baby joeys are often frisky and jump away from their mothers as they stretch their legs. Have all the girls be baby joeys and have them hop around the play area. The boys then hop to try and tag a joey and bring her home again. Once a mother kangaroo has tagged a joey, they must hop together to the side of the play area. The mother kangaroo can return to the game to help catch other hopping joeys. Once all the joeys have been caught, switch places and let the boys be the joeys and have the girls hop after them.

[4] Roll and Jump

Have the children guess how many times they can jump. Have each child roll a pair of dice and see if he can hop or jump the number indicated on the dice. Have each child roll and count while he jumps. After everyone has had a chance to roll and jump, team the children up with a partner. Have each partner challenge the other to a jumping duel. The first partner chooses a number of jumps to challenge the second player. Both partners count and jump the number of times challenged by the first partner. Swap places and have the second child issue the jumping challenge to the first.

[4-5] Hopscotch

Using sidewalk chalk, let the children draw hopscotch diagrams by drawing a series of numbered boxes stacked on top of one another on the sidewalk. They can choose any number of squares to add to their hopscotch path. Starting at the first box numbered "1," have the child toss a beanbag into a square and jump into each square, counting each number as they jump to the end of the boxes. (Skip the box with the beanbag.) As they return to the start, remind them to pick up their beanbag on the way back. Have them take turns tossing and jumping with a friend.